FOREW

So you said yes to serving the kids of your church - way to go legend! I'll never forget when I said yes, I was in my early 20's and I didn't know the first thing about ministering to kids. I was a worship leader in our youth ministry getting ready for service when my pastor showed up and said nineteen words that changed my life forever, "Grab your guitar and your bible and go to children's church. The lady who runs the class is missing."(I still to this day don't know what happened to her, we never saw her again, she could still be missing for all I know.) I don't recall ever really saying yes, I just went, because my pastor needed help. If I only knew, how saying yes would change my life's direction and God's plan for my life I wouldn't have felt so inadequate. I didn't have a clue what to do or how to effectively minister to kids, I just knew yes was the right answer. I just knew the Bible was plain, JESUS LOVES KIDS! There was nothing for me to read or study, there was nothing to show me what I didn't know and I didn't know what I didn't know to ask the right questions. I learned the hard way by learning as I walked out ministry, and by making mistakes.

Fast forward four decades, I'm in my early sixties, there are a lot of books on children's ministry leadership, books on the theories and principles behind ministry to children. There are more resources and curriculums than ever before. Most growing churches see the importance of reaching kids at a young age and training them to be the church now, but there's not been a practical guide that you can read to teach you what you don't know about serving with more passion, purpose and with greater longevity until now.

IF ONLY YOU KNEW is a game changer for those new to serving the kids of your church. Thanks Dave, for once again being obedient to the Lord and for allowing Him to use you in meeting a much-needed need. This book will help you to build lives and help you thrive in reaching this next generation.

Jim Wideman
Kidmin Pioneer and Family Pastor
at The Belonging Company, Nashville, TN

INTRODUCTION.

Last year I visited India with my 10 year old son. We went to see my parents who run an orphanage in the Northwest of the country - but we started in Mumbai.

Talk about a culture shock. India is an incredibly different place to my home in Sydney, Australia. The people, the noise, the smell... "Holy Cow!" I said as we almost ran over one relaxing in the middle of the road. I was in a different world, with different rules and expectations. A different language and people. I was an immigrant in a new culture.

The most effective missionaries learn the language, the culture and build bridges. They don't come in and impose their own values and ideas upon an unsuspecting people.

That's how I want you to see yourself as you enter the world of kids - an immigrant, a missionary into an unknown culture. Come in humbly, without agenda, just seeking to learn and grow - eventually you will become a local, a guide for others into this mysterious new culture.

Let me say this another way; You are not here to 'bring Jesus' to your group of kids. You are here to seek out and discover exactly what God is already doing in their lives and join **WITH** Him in ministry.

India opened my eyes to see that the way I live is not the only way to follow Jesus. It showed me, though our differences are large, at the centre of it all, we are people, in different kinds of families, seeking to follow one God.

These two principles are where it all begins - I cannot stress enough just how important they are.

- You are a missionary.
- You are joining with what Jesus is already doing.

This attitude of being a missionary changes the way you see the world for the better. As you start this journey of ministry to children, be aware it is the biggest harvest field in the world. Right now children (15 and below) make up 27% of the population of earth - that's 1.9 billion young people!

Population experts estimate we have reached the peak number of children, which means this is the most amount of children earth may ever see alive at one time.[1]

This is our moment, our opportunity to join with Jesus in seeing this generation follow Him!

1 Max Roser and Esteban Ortiz-Ospina (2017) – 'World Population Growth'. Published online at www.ourworldindata.org Retrieved from: https://ourworldindata.org/world-population-growth/ [Online Resource]

ONE.

HOW DID YOU END UP HERE?

He that takes truth for his guide, and duty for his end, may safely trust to God's providence to lead him aright.

—Blaise Pascal

Movies have a way of distorting reality. Simple situations can appear much harder than they really are, and incredibly complex situations can seem overly simple.

For example, changing a nappy/diaper. Every day millions of babies all over the world have their soiled nappies successfully removed, bottom talcum powdered, and nappy dutifully replaced... No big deal, just parents doing what they gotta do. It's not enjoyable, but it's far more enjoyable than having to deal with a rash that keeps your precious nugget awake until 3am.

But to watch a movie with a nappy-changing scene is to witness the notion that changing a baby is the most traumatic event you could possibly participate in. It seems like there will be explosions of numerous body fluids on a daily basis and when all is said and done, you will have to burn the clothes you were wearing because of the devastating ordeal of what just occurred.

It's not 'that' bad.

On the flipside, movies also tend to make complex situations appear simple, like the ease with which a seven year old armed only with a laptop and a cell phone from 1993, can hack into the missile launch computer of an evil mastermind and prevent a nuclear disaster with a few rapid clicks on a keyboard.

Stories you've heard about children's ministry probably face that similar distortion. You could easily imagine facing vomit on a weekly basis, parents wielding pitchforks, hospital emergency room visits and preschool gangs roaming the hall looking for victims.

It's not that bad... close... but not that bad.

Full disclosure:
1. 'Code Brown' is a real thing
2. Being covered in slime for the amusement of preteens is a real possibility.

What I have come to discover over time is that serving the children of your church is largely whatever you make of it. To stay passionate every week means living with an expectation that God had something to say to each group of children, in each church service.

This group of children isn't the same as the one from last service, and they each have something unique both to contribute and receive.

It's being willing to see the spark in the team you are serving with, the needs of the kids you are ministering to, and the wisdom to realise that the time it takes for this church service to happen has the potential to create a moment that everyone involved will never forget.

There are moments growing up in church I will never forget. For some reason I remember watching 'Star Trek IV: The Voyage Home', you know the one with the time travelling whale in space. But along with the good times, I also recall getting lines to write for misbehaving from one of the volunteers...

This is not a good idea
This is not a good idea
This is not a...

As a leader I am happy if the children I serve have memories like this (well, apart from the lines), but I truly believe that you and I can be part of memories of God moving in miraculous ways and children being transformed by Christ.

> "My dear children, for whom I am again in the pains of childbirth until Christ is FORMED in you..." Galatians 4:19 (NIV)

> "And we all, who with unveiled faces contemplate the Lord's glory, are being transformed into his image with ever-increasing glory, which comes from the Lord, who is the Spirit." 2 Corinthians 3:18 (NIV)

This is the goal, this is the prize. This is the reason I still get excited thinking about this high calling to serve children. But enough about me - how did you get here?

How did you discover this crazy world of people serving in kidmin?

There are various reasons I have observed over the years for why people get involved.

Called: You feel a certain pull that might be Jesus revealing what He has for your future.

Pleaded: There was an act of desperation, and you ended up serving on team.

Volunteered: There was a need, and you put your hand up to give your energy and time.

Bamboozled: The old bait and switch... "We just need you for a short term, a few weeks at the most" (that was two years ago).

Or maybe this book has just appeared in your hands... surprise! Welcome to the team.

No matter how you got here and why you are reading this book, I want to ignite in you a passion for this season of your life.

God isn't just looking for the development of faith in the kids you serve. He wants to see Christ formed in you as well!

I truly believe that your development is right at the front of His mind.

Talking practically, you can get better at what you do. Unequivocally I am 'better' at running a small group for kids than the leader who has been on team for 3 weeks. Did that happen overnight? No. But it did happen, and my mission is to improve my skill level at whatever opportunity comes my way.

So what skills are you going to develop while being a part of children's ministry?

- Public speaking
- Group facilitation
- Time management
- Delegation
- Conflict management ("I was playing with that first!")
- Inspiring others
- Communication
- Team building
- Mentoring
- Collaboration
- People skills
- Organisation
- Vision casting

And... like it or not, the names of at least 23 YouTubers.

These are skills that will help you navigate your ministry world, your workplace, your school, pretty much any circumstance you find yourself in. What I'm really saying is, bring on the 'zombie apocalypse,' kidmin leaders will be ready for it!

Really, it's all what you make of it, but throwing yourself into this ministry can uncover gifts and talents you never knew you had.

P.S. Before I return you to your regularly scheduled programming, do you know your spiritual giftings and strengths? If not, FIND OUT! Don't live another day without knowing.[2]

---

2 Highly recommend is Strengths Finder. (www.strengthsfinder.com)

TWO.

WHAT'S THE DEAL WITH KIDS?

One generation shall commend Your works to another,
and shall declare Your mighty acts.

Psalm 145:4 (ESV)

I was worried about the amount of screen time my kids were getting.

Like all parents, I imagined my life as a child was spent running free amongst fields replete with amber waves of grain, while today's generation maintains a sedentary lifestyle fuelled by TV, white sugar and sour gummies.

When my son bought himself a fitness tracker, I realised I had been worrying for no reason. The sheer amount of exercise (up to 30,000 steps) he was getting everyday obliterated my concern that 'kids these days' sat at home playing video games.

Every generation tends to look at the generation coming up with disdain. An article in Time magazine claimed "seventy-one percent of American adults think of 18 to 29 year-olds — millennials, basically — as 'selfish,' and sixty-five percent think of them as 'entitled.'"[3]

But misunderstandings between generations have been going on since the beginning of language.

There is a 4,000 year old cave painting in Patagonia that palaeontologists believe was drawn by a 13 year old. It translates roughly "My parents... Ugh! I can't even...". Underneath is simply a picture of a WiFi symbol with a red line through it.

Be careful, older human people, not to focus on good behaviour as the end goal. Sure, we all want a calm and peaceful environment that enables distraction-free learning, but there will always be a gap between our experience and our desire. Of all the ministries in the Church, serving our kids might just be the most unpredictable.

We have a short time each weekend to minister to kids, maybe sixty to ninety minutes, and it's vital we take advantage of every moment. Think about it this way -- if you add up all the time we spend with kids in a year, it will still be less than a week at school. Which means our

3 From TIME.com © 2013 TIME USA LLC. All rights Reserved. Used under License.
TIME.com and TIME USA LLC. Are not affiliated with, and do not endorse products or services of, Hillsong Church.

short term behaviour management techniques will simply not bring about transformation.

Even the term 'behaviour management' is unhelpful. God did not give us children to manage but support. You aren't called to tell children **WHAT** they should and shouldn't be doing but remind them **WHO** they are and have the potential to become. You are aiming for a heart connection, because as you may have heard it said, no one cares how much you know until they know how much you care.

I remember promising myself as a teenager that I would never forget what it was like to be young. I would intentionally resist the march of time on my youthful mind but now, decades later I find myself enjoying TV shows about antiques and napping in the afternoon.

It takes a deliberate force of my will to put myself in the shoes of a child and remember to give them grace, maybe let some attitudes and moments slide and remember to do for one what you wish you could do for all.

Don't be overwhelmed by the needs of all your kids and as a result, do nothing. You may not be able to help everyone, but you can help one. I can give to **ONE**, the way I wish I could do for everyone.

I heard Pastor Andy Stanley[4] talk about this principle. He continued by talking about a phrase I think you have heard before. "If I let you do it, I have to let **EVERYONE** do it!" or maybe "If I give you one, I have to give everyone one."

Every time I heard this from my parents or a teacher, I would think, "Uhh, no you don't. I won't tell anyone if you don't!"

This phrase is about control. It teaches that since you can't do it for everyone, you won't do it for one and so nothing gets done.

Instead, DO FOR ONE WHAT WE WISH WE COULD DO FOR EVERYONE. The question is, "Who's the one?"

- Who is the one child you can help?
- Which child needs an encouraging word?
- Who do you hear from the least, maybe the introverted personalities?

Children face very different challenges in this current generation, but in some ways they need the same things they have always needed: Love, encouragement, ice-cream... and when you are together with them they need you to 'give away the ministry'.

"Tell me, I'll forget. Show me, I'll remember. Involve me, I'll understand."

—Chinese proverb.

GIVE AWAY THE MINISTRY

By taking on this awesome task of serving the kids of your church, you have received an opportunity. That's great, but it shouldn't stop there; you need to create opportunities.

Check out what Jesus got His disciples to do:

> "When Jesus had called the Twelve together, he gave them power and authority to drive out all demons and to cure diseases, and he sent them out to proclaim the kingdom of God and to heal the sick. He told them: "Take nothing for the journey—no staff, no bag, no bread, no money, no extra shirt. Whatever house you enter, stay there until you leave that town. If people do not welcome you, leave their town and shake the dust off your feet as a testimony against them." So they set out and went from village to village, proclaiming the good news and healing people everywhere." Luke 9:1-6 (NIV)

Firstly, Jesus gave His followers the opportunity to do what He did.

Everything Jesus was asking them to do they had seen Him do time and time again, there were no hidden surprises. But this was not just an object lesson where Jesus expects them to fail and come back with their tails between their legs, saying, "I don't know how you do it Jesus. You're awesome. I could never be like you."

I don't see Jesus setting anyone up for terrible failure. His disciples had a lot to learn, but our New Testament wouldn't exist if they hadn't succeeded.

> "Very truly I tell you, whoever believes in me will do the works I have been doing, and they will do even greater things than these, because I am going to the Father." John 14:12 (NIV)

Your church wouldn't exist if the Church hadn't spread to every corner of the earth.

The more I see church life in action, the more I see the absolute necessity of giving kids what the educational world calls 'agency'.

Agency is defined as being able to make choices and decisions to influence events and to have an impact on one's world. It doesn't matter if you are a full time pastor or a volunteer who just had their first Sunday last week, seeing kids participate fully in your church community is your lofty goal.

But we need to take it one level further.

Secondly, Jesus gave the disciples responsibility AND authority.

One of the biggest video games of the last few years is Minecraft. Players have complete autonomy to create a world shaped by their imagination. Every decision and choice is theirs. Can you imagine children saying that about your church?

In a time where children can create content seen by kids all over the globe, see your church through **their** eyes. Is it a space where they are told to sit still and listen while adults talk?

Or are they presented every week with an opportunity to serve, to lead, to make choices, decisions and initiate their own learning? The kingdom of God is alive with opportunity -- and you have the power to give it to them.

Responsibility can be easy: "Can you please run the sound desk today? Can you push play on the DVD player?" But the idea of giving kids authority is nothing if not daunting.

But imagine a child growing up in a church where he is responsible for and has the authority to participate in the direction of what the ministry to his peers needs to be!

I believe a church who gives their children responsibility and authority will change the future.

> "But Jesus called them to Himself and said, "You know that the rulers of the Gentiles lord it over them, and those who are great exercise authority over them. Yet it shall not be so among you; but whoever desires to become great among you, let him be your servant. And whoever desires to be first among you, let him be your slave — just as the Son of Man did not come to be served, but to serve, and to give His life a ransom for many." Matthew 20:25-28 (NKJV)

Jesus didn't tell us **NOT** to be great. He told us to **BE** great... by serving.

Your mission is to offer children the opportunity to be servants.

Here's the last paragraph of the Time Magazine article I mentioned at the beginning of this chapter.

> "...A generation's greatness isn't determined by data; it's determined by how they react to the challenges that befall them. And, just as important, by how we react to them. Whether you think millennials are the new greatest generation of optimistic entrepreneurs or a group of 80 million people about to implode in a dwarf star of tears when their expectations are unmet depends largely on how you view change. Me, I choose to believe in the children. God knows they do."[5]

I too choose to have hope and expectation, believing like so many before us that Jesus will continue to build His Church.

THREE.

GIFTY MCGIFTERSON

We know the excitement of getting a present - we love to unwrap it to see what is inside. So it is with our children they are gifts we unwrap for years as we discover the unique characters God has made them.

—Cornelius Plantinga

Curiosity started at an early age for me. I wanted to see how things worked; disassembling them was part of that process. Unfortunately, putting them back together proved a challenge for both my frustrated parents and me.

I left a trail of unassembled objects around our house, but I needed to know how things worked, even if that meant destroying them!

Now, I want to know how YOU tick.

I'm not going to take you apart, but let me quote myself from chapter one:

"...Do you know your spiritual giftings and strengths? If not, FIND OUT! Don't live another day without knowing."

If you work in business, government, education or health care, you have probably been exposed to the ongoing strengths movement. Which is the idea that you'll gain more by improving your strengths, than spending time fixing your weaknesses.

The Bible backs this approach up.

"God has given each of you a gift from his great variety of spiritual gifts. Use them well to serve one another." 1 Peter 4:10 (NLT)

"There are diversities of gifts, but the same Spirit." 1 Corinthians 12:4 (NKJV)

If you have ever hired someone, you understand job interviews are not about accomplishments and qualifications. A successful applicant tells the potential employer what they will add to the organisation.

God knows exactly what you are going to add to His Church. He is excited about the plans and purpose in your future and would love to let you know about it. So I have said before and I will say it again: investigate, research and come to an understanding of what makes you tick!

But here's the thing...

Joel 3:10 (NKJV) finishes with the phrase, "Let the weak say I am strong," or in the New Living Translation version, "Train even your weaklings to be warriors." Our Saviour is very fond of turning the world as we know it on its head. What we think we know may turn out to be the exact opposite in the Kingdom of God.

The weak are strong, the poor are rich, the meek shall inherit the earth... what's going on here?

Check out this verse from the Apostle Paul:

> "I came to you in weakness with great fear and trembling. My message and my preaching were not with wise and persuasive words, but with a demonstration of the Spirit's power, so that your faith might not rest on human wisdom, but on God's power." 1 Corinthians 2:3-5 (NIV)

I am not naturally a pastor. Sure, it's in my job description, but let's have a look at my strengths.

- Futuristic
- Ideation
- Intellection
- Learner
- Belief

I'm always thinking about the future. I love innovation and new ideas. I examine my thought processes and hunt for evidence to support my theories. I yearn to be inspired by my work and try to be helpful to others in ways that may improve their lives.

Now, what's missing in that list of strengths?

Only one has to do with people.

Ha, God. You funny...

The other strengths are about strategic thinking, which is great for planning but doesn't exactly make me a caring, shepherding, lover of others. However, it is what God has called me to do and since I started this journey 15 years ago, one thing is very clear to me: I have had to rely on the strength that Christ has given me every day.

That verse in the book of Joel is so relevant to my journey. Let the weak say I am strong - it's a daily reminder that I need Him in everything I do.

> "Seeing then that we have a great High Priest who has passed through the heavens, Jesus the Son of God, let us hold fast our confession." Hebrews 4:14 (NKJV)

I have no doubt the reason I still have a job is because I have embraced my weaknesses. I need God's grace and His power to live out this calling!

But enough about me.

Working with children is not a gift. It's the gift you bring to the table that helps you live out this adventure.

You might be an expert in executing. You know how to make things happen; you can 'catch' an idea and make it a reality.

You might be the relationship builder, the essential glue that holds teams together. You could have the ability to create groups that accomplish more together than apart.

Or perhaps you are a strategic thinker, focussing everyone on what could be, helping the team make better decisions, and stretching thinking for the future.

And then there are influencers, you bring others on the journey. You take charge, speak up and make sure your team is heard.

> "Keep watch over yourselves and all the flock of which the Holy Spirit has made you overseers. Be shepherds of the church of God, which he bought with his own blood." Acts 20:28 (NIV)

Paul went so far as to boast in his weakness:

> "...but I will not boast about myself, except about my weaknesses." 2 Corinthians 12:5 (NIV)

Can you boast in your weakness? Can you operate in your strength?

I hate wasting people's time, especially the time of a volunteer. Church is all about God and people, and I want the process to get out of the way so ministry takes its place. I want the same for you. I want you to be fulfilled in your ministry. I want you to operate at a world class level, which means you **NEED** to be operating in your strengths and trusting God to help you in your weaknesses.

Christianity is impossible if it's up to you. We need Christ and when it comes to your ministry, you need to need Him.

FOUR.

ARE YOU WINNING?

We should not judge people by their peak of excellence; but by the distance they have traveled from the point where they started.

—Henry Ward Beecher

"Incoming," he yelled, the fear and panic evident in his voice. Time slowed as around the corner came the horde. Eyes wide, white knuckles, sweat beading on every creased forehead. Were they ready? In one corner sat a fresh faced young recruit rocking back and forth in a small ball while whispering, "yea though I walk through the valley of the shadow..."

It was about to start all over again... Sunday morning.

In most churches, Sunday is the main event. Perhaps you have one or two services morning and night, or even more. The record in my own church is nine services over Saturday night and Sunday morning in one location (I know what you're thinking: "I can't wait for that to happen in my church!").

It was a short season and in the brief moments between services as the dust would settle it would cross my mind frequently, "Was that a 'good' service?"

I understand that God is much bigger than what we can comprehend or understand and it is ridiculous to think we can manufacture what only Jesus can do. But as we see in the Bible time and time again, God works through people just like you and me.

So, how do you define a 'win'? What do you consider a success?

My goal is to give you the ability to articulate what you and your team consider a great Sunday. Before you read any further, I would like you to prepare your pen for a short exercise. Don't read past it or sneak a look.

Write down three wins that would make you feel like you had a great weekend:

1. _____

_____

2. _____

_____

3. _____

_____

I know a mere .02% have actually written something down, half of you are upset that I would even dare suggest writing in this masterpiece of literature, and the other half are just simply offended that I would dare tell you what to do.

I know - I'm angry at myself for even suggesting it! The nerve of me!

I have no way of knowing what you wrote down unless you tweet at me @davewakerley. However, I do know some of you may not have any idea what to write. If you're one of those people, I'd like to talk to you right now.

Think back to your childhood, especially if you grew up in Church. What are the moments you can remember? What are things that stick out in your mind?

I grew up in a small town with about 600 people - we had 150 kids in our school. The church my family was a part of was huge, or so I thought, but looking back it may have been significantly smaller than I remember. The church's kids ministry was upstairs. Along with bright red carpet, it had a TV, a VCR, and smaller rooms for each age group. The place was full of amazing people who loved God.

Because of them, I have fond memories of my time there.

I dare say that the kids you lead today may have a similar experience (likely without a VCR). They will hopefully remember some big events or important moments but, don't expect them to recall your preaching points from March 7, 2011.

The leader that consistently sows into the lives of others has a place in the hearts and minds of those they serve. Look out for milestones and growth no matter how small in the people around you.

Here are some things I really want to accomplish during a weekend:

Take a deep dive into 'Kid Culture' - Showing kids you care is easy. Over the years, I have had many conversations about things I knew nothing about: The complete history of certain collectable trading card games for example, and I know way more than I ever expected to know about the video game Minecraft - be interested not just interesting.

Have a spiritual conversation - It's simply bringing God into the middle of a problem. Prayer is often the last resort rather than the first option, so my mission during a weekend is to engage with kids, pinpoint their needs, and invite Jesus into the situation.

Speak a word of encouragement to a child - Seize the moment and in front of all the kids or during small group time, take the time to remind a child that God knows them by name.

Make kids laugh - It's important we make Church a place that is enjoyed, not just endured. The simple fact is if kids are having fun, they are learning. Defences are down and worries, forgotten. This is not optional. It's part of the reason why our curriculum videos contain so much comedy.

Give away the ministry - Can I give an opportunity for someone else to take the lead? Can I empower someone else to try something they have never done before? If I notice someone is gifted in an area, I want to do everything in my power to develop that gift.

But at the end of the day it's important to note that I don't just do what I think is important.

As a vital part of your church team, you don't function as an island. In a healthy team, people are connected and support each other. Doing only what you think is important is a surefire way to frustration.

I want to fulfil the mission statement of our church, not build a separate ministry.

What do your Pastor and leadership team value? What would they consider a win? Ask them the question - you might be surprised by the answer. It may just redirect your efforts to something greater than you could have imagined.

FIVE.

MORE?

When I consider my ministry, I think of the world. Anything less than that would not be worthy of Christ, nor of his will for my life.

—Henrietta C. Mears

Growing up I didn't realise Children's Ministry was 'a thing.' I knew that our church had kids in it sure, but as for what happened with them during church... no idea. That all changed when I started Bible College in Sydney. As part of my studies, I started serving in the life of our church. As fate would have it, I was assigned to the kids ministry and began on the Saturday night team. It was a revelation and by the end of the service, I had the microphone and was up at the front, talking to the kids. From that day in February 2001 until today, serving the children of our church is what I do week in and week out.

It only took a short time before I wanted more. I felt like I had something to offer the ministry, so I began to see needs and fill them. A few months later, an opportunity to oversee the kids worship team was offered to me - saying 'Yes' put me on the path I still find myself on today.

Music albums, TV shows, videos, curriculum, building into the lives of families... It all came from a 'yes' to flying to another country for Bible College, a 'yes' to serving with children, a 'yes' to leading a worship team.

Reading this book right now, you may feel exactly like that. You see a need and cannot wait to get involved and contribute, make a difference, fix something! On the other hand, you might have been given this book to read and still find yourself overwhelmed and confused at the beginning of chapter five.

I get it — I'm talking about 'doing more' and you are still at the corner of 'Just started' and 'What the heck is that for?'

To answer that I need to talk about puberty.

The best time to talk to your children about dating is years before they even consider it. Before my eldest son reached his 11th birthday, we went on a two day retreat and talked about all the changes he was about to experience. It was an amazing time, we prayed together and spent time to 'Decide in Advance' some of the boundaries and resolutions he would keep in the intense season of teenage hood.

Which is why I feel like I would do you a disservice if I didn't bring up the future. Of course, we won't talk about the birds and the bees - that would be weird -- but I do want to enforce the power of preparing for the future. When we walk with God, the best is yet to come.

> "...I am certain that God, who began the good work within you, will continue his work until it is finally finished on the day when Christ Jesus returns." Philippians 1:6 (NLT)

It's just possible, almost certain, God will use this next season of your life as a springboard to your future. There are dreams in your heart you want to see come to pass and right now the greatest commitment you could have is to take every opportunity enthusiastically.

> "Whatever your hand finds to do, do it with your might; for there is no work or device or knowledge or wisdom in the grave where you are going." Ecclesiastes 9:10 (NKJV)

Children's ministry can present itself as a lifetime mission. However, putting that pressure on a new volunteer can overwhelm them, accomplishing the opposite goal.

Right now, I'm in this for life. I have committed myself to God. He determines my steps. My allegiance is to a Saviour, not a system, a Messiah, not a method. Following Jesus is a journey into the unknown -- I like the mystery.

For those of you serving in children's ministry, know your pastor, your leaders are more excited than a tornado in a trailer park to have you serve. They see your potential and the opportunities your service provides their local church.

They also believe you matter more than the job you do. Businesses recruit but families adopt -- so my prayer for you is that you would find a home in your team and as you serve, let this be your prayer:

"Restore to me the joy of your salvation and grant me a willing spirit, to sustain me." Psalm 51:12 (NIV)

For now, rest in the wisdom found in Proverbs;

"Commit to the Lord whatever you do, and he will establish your plans." Proverbs 16:3 (NIV)

WHAT CAN I DO?

As I mentioned before, the main event for most churches is the weekend service. But if you find yourself with the availability to serve outside of weekend services and take on another area of ministry, there are other things you can do to get more involved.

In the area of administration: Sending birthday cards to the kids in your church, data entry, weekend preparation; craft, activities, small group preparation.

For those with a pastoral heart: Following up visiting families from the weekend, weekly mentoring, schools ministry, preaching preparation.

Creatives could help out with: Curriculum writing, video production, praise and worship preparation, script writing, songwriting, project management, graphic design.

Every team needs people gifted in Communications: Weekend rosters, social media management, team emails.

Your gifts and talents may be jumping up and down with excitement at the thought of contributing to one of these areas. If you have the availability and capacity, don't wait for someone to request your involvement. Humbly approach the right people with your idea, being open and willing to lightly hold your expectations.

Even if this isn't your 'first rodeo' and you have been around the ministry block once or twice, keep Joshua in mind;

> "I am as strong this day as on the day that Moses sent me... therefore, give me this mountain of which the Lord spoke..." Joshua 14:11-12 (NKJV)

Whatever your mountain, and whatever the 'more' looks like for you, have this conviction in your heart:

The future can be better than today's reality, and I have the power to make that happen.

I spent the later part of the 80's with a guy called Mario and his brother Luigi, trying to rescue a princess who had been kidnapped by a guy named Bowser. It took me many weeks to beat world one. When I reached the first castle and thought the game was over, the game presented me with seven more worlds to conquer.

Dear Reader, Christ said He would build the Church, and your local gathering of believers is a part of it. Don't miss out on the 'worlds' that await you.

Remember '...the princess is in another castle'. (Thanks Mario)

SIX.

LASTING THE DISTANCE

You teach a little by what you say.
You teach the most by what you are.

—Henrietta C. Mears

I sat across from one of the most accomplished surgeons in Australia while he told me how he planned to remove the tumour that had made its home in my body.

I was 38.

And this was not in my calendar.

One hour later, I found myself on a Sydney beach, drenched with salt water as I pounded a wooden stake into the shore and re-enacted the story of the man who built his house on the sand for a short film.

The surreal moment was heightened by the reality of my circumstance.

Cancer before the age of 40.

Since I was a child, the church has told me to build my life on the rock, Jesus Christ, the Son of God.

Here was my test.

Was my house built on solid rock? Or was I about to crumble and sink slowly into the sand?

On the other side of that trial, I can say one thing for certain: I didn't know what the future held but at no point did I doubt my calling.

Believing God has things for you to do in the future helps you cling to hope in a powerful way.

Because of the heritage of faith I received as a child, just like those three ancient heroes Shadrach, Meshach and Abednego in the book of Daniel, I was able to say that my God was willing and able to save, but even if He doesn't... I still choose to stand on that rock.

Will the child you encourage this weekend stand strong?

With your life, example and faith, point children to the Rock. Tell them the story of your struggle, pain and storm. In each church service, the minutes you spend with kids are the building materials constructing a house on stone.

I've seen the lives built on sand -- the friend whose faith evaporated in the first semester of University when confronted with a professor's perspective of reality, the family that faded away from the church as they negotiated a divorce.

This season of your life may be a marathon or it may be a 100 metre sprint, only time will tell. How you start is important... and how you finish is important.

Jesus expects believers to put their hand to the plough (Luke 9:62). He wants us to commit fully to whatever is ahead of us.

Sometimes you plough a field full of rocks and sometimes you plough and the soil is loose, fertile and ready for planting. You can't control the soil. You can only work with what you have.

God promises us fruitfulness, if you simply keep doing good and don't give up.

I want you to flourish. The harvest is ripe. The Gospel of Jesus is needed in every nation, tongue and tribe. However, as I mentioned in an earlier chapter, you matter more than the job you do.

The dashboard of your life has a bunch of gauges that need to be monitored. Adjustments must be made to keep you in the race.

Great men and women have been taken out by destructive behaviours and attitudes. I pay attention to these symptoms. With the energy required to effectively serve children, I hope you will watch for these problematic signs, too.

There are many studies that focus on the pressures of full-time ministry, books written on burnout, and resources to help those who feel overwhelmed by their calling. In the Unites States alone, statistics show that 1,500 pastors leave their ministries each month due to burnout, conflict, or moral failure.[6]

But dropping out is not just about the 'professionals,' it's about the volunteer giving time and energy to a cause greater than themselves. It's about navigating life so you succeed in every sphere: work, play, family, ministry... every area.

When the oil light comes up on your dashboard don't ignore it. When the fuel gauge lights up as it dips towards empty, grab some gas. These indicators are a signal it's time to make a change. Refuel, change the oil, put air in the tyres — do something, because if you don't the consequences are going to be painful.

There are certain gauges I think volunteers need to monitor.

Joy — it's the emotional gauge. Warning signs: Can you describe your main emotion as numbness? Do you not experience excitement or feel the lows? Seeing a child engage with the Word of God should be something that fills your heart with joy.

Participation — It's the motivation gauge. When a meeting is announced, has your response turned from "I get to do this!" to "Do I have to do this?" If you find yourself asking the 'have to' question, it's a sign that something deeper is going on.

6 H.B. London and Neil B. Wiseman.
(2003) Leaders at Greater Risk, Rev. Ed. Ventura, CA: Regal Books

Attitude — It's the cynicism gauge. Warning signs: Do you doubt if those around you are genuine? Maybe you wonder what the happy, smiley people are hiding.

Cynicism has no place in a happy heart.

The Church of Jesus needs you to be healthy. If you ever hear my own Senior Pastor Brian Houston preach, there is a strong possibility he will talk about the condition of the heart. It's a major theme in his preaching that comes out especially when he is talking to leaders. He knows from experience the heart is your most important leadership tool.

> "Keep your heart with all diligence, For out of it spring the issues of life." Proverbs 4:23 (NJKV)

In 1996 Dr. Billy Graham and his wife, Ruth, received the Congressional Gold Medal - the highest honour which the US Government can bestow on a civilian. Only 263 individuals, at that time, had ever received it. In his acceptance speech, Dr. Graham spoke about his team.

> "As we read the list of the distinguished Americans who have received the congressional gold medal in the past, beginning with George Washington in 1776, we know we do not belong in this same company. And we feel very unworthy. One reason is we both know that this honour ought to be shared with those who have helped us over the years... our ministry has been a team effort. And without our associates and our family, we could never have accomplished anything."[7]

This is a man who worked with a tightly knit ministry team for 45 years and recognised the success he had seen was due to the men and women around him.

7 Billy Graham ©1996 The Billy Graham Literary Trust

It was demonstrated most powerfully but he fact that many of his close team in the later years remained living closely together in North Carolina... let's be honest, you only do that after 45 years if you really like someone.

I hope that my life is surrounded with the people God has put in my life, the team that has not only fulfilled the call of God, but remained friends. The team who still like each other through all the ups and downs, twists and turns of life and ministry. Still caring and supporting each other through hip replacements, hearing loss and increased fibre consumption.

You only get to a place like that if you protect your heart — and no other club or group has such a potential to change lives like the house of God you are building, nothing even comes close. A body, as Jesus calls us, a living breathing expression of Heaven on earth.

"His house is the tangible framework that embraces and cherishes His people which then causes them to flourish in life" - Bobbie Houston.[8]

8 Bobbie Houston *Heaven is in this House*, Maximised Leadership Inc. 2001.

SEVEN.

HERE'S WHAT YOU ARE INVOLVED IN

A church begins to die when it says, 'They were just children'.

—Wess Stafford

Nothing frustrates me more than putting time and energy into an idea that is going nowhere and I think it's safe to say you feel the same way. Everyone wants to know what they do is making a difference.

The simple reason I am committed to my local church is because I believe it's the greatest catalyst to see change in the world.

But why children?

I think Wess Stafford, former CEO of Compassion International, says it best:

"Every major movement in world history has recognized the strategic importance of mobilizing children. The Nazis had their Hitler Youth bands. The Chinese Communists had their Red Guards. The Taliban in Afghanistan had their madrash schools to instill extremism in the young. The great omission seems to be unique to Christians."[9]

My family sponsors several children around the world through Compassion Australia. According to Compassion International, here's why Compassion focuses on kids:

During Compassion's 60-plus years of development work, we've seen various approaches to breaking the cycle of poverty in children's lives. We've discovered that changed circumstances rarely change people's lives, while changed people inevitably change their circumstances. Community development is important work that addresses the external circumstances of poverty and is an important complement to our work. However, our primary focus is individual child development—an inside-out, bottom-up approach that recognizes the God-given value and potential of each individual child. Many of these children grow up to become positive influences in their own communities.[10]

9 Wess Stafford and Dean Merrill, *Too Small to Ignore: Why Children are the Next Big Thing,* Colorado Springs: Waterbrook Press, 2005. 7.

10 Compassion International. Available: https://www.compassion.com/about/faq.htm

This wisdom applies to you and me as we prepare to serve our ministries this weekend. We have before us, shining in the eyes of our children, a glimpse of Jesus. They are so often a people without a voice, but they are also the agents for great change in the world.

They are not the Church of tomorrow.

They are the Church of today.

My goal for this book is simple. By the time you finish reading it, I pray you'll be prepared in a greater way to serve the kids of your local church and have the revelation that kids are in the centre of God's plan for earth.

You can't be a parent to every child in your care but as you build relationships, you serve by supporting, affirming, and adding to the faith of our children. You're not doing the task alone. You have the helper, the Holy Spirit to show what the kids need from you most.

Don't lead out of fear.

I know there are statistics that show the abandoning of Christianity by a younger generation. However, worry and fear are not going to help you be more effective in your ministry. Instead, have faith God will finish what He started.

> "being confident of this very thing, that He who has begun a good work in you will complete it until the day of Jesus Christ" Philippians 1:6 (NKJV)

At the end of each Hillsong church service, it's common for someone to say thanks to those in attendance. The gratitude comes out of the hearts of our Senior Pastors who appreciate the individuals that compose our community.

Maybe you need to hear a "thank you" right now.

Thank you.

Thanks for saying yes.

> "Beloved, I pray that you may prosper in all things and be in health, just as your soul prospers." 3 John 2 (NKJV)

You need to prosper. It's the surest way for you to fully step into the work God has prepared for you.

HERE'S WHAT YOU ARE INVOLVED IN:

- A ministry with a Holy calling, an influence that is eternal.

- A ministry with a clear mission too vital to be ignored.

- A ministry where we are to speak up for those who cannot speak for themselves.

- Your Senior Pastor has entrusted the children of your church community to you.

- You have committed yourself to see a generation grow in the grace and knowledge of Christ Jesus.

- You are part of a team that the families of or our church trust.

- They trust you to reinforce and underpin the message of the Gospel of Jesus Christ to their kids.

- You make church a safe place.

- You make church meaningful.

- You make church fun.

- You create the space for every child to experience God and participate in His kingdom.

- Let the Church get the blessing and God get the glory.

- You are a minister. You minister to the largest mission field in the world.

You minister to children.

APPENDIX 1: FORMATIONAL THOUGHTS

I want to highlight the work of a number of leaders in Australia as part of the Here2Stay.org initiative[11]. I present to you the 8 pillars of formation that lead to transformation in the lives of children. Assess your current ministry and how each of these concepts appear in the life of your Church.

1. Anchors/Rites of passage: ☐/10

Many cultures are rich in significant events acknowledging a young person's growth and development. How do we help a young person navigate these experiences? How can we be more strategic and intentional with our kids? What can we do to create spaces and anchors to help them transform?

2. Mentors and life coaches: ☐/10

Questions arise every day, small and large, about how life works and why it doesn't work. Close, warm relationships are vital when exploring strange, sometimes threatening territory, asking some of life's biggest questions.

3. Peak experiences: ☐/10

A peak experience is a vital complement to the regular activities within the faith community. The experience may be a residential camp, a day camp, a special Saturday program, a concert, a special evening program, and so on. In these contexts, faith is deepened through the mixture of meeting new people with a real faith, being inspired by new leaders with a vibrant faith, living in community, the 'wow' factor of a bigger or special event.

11 HERE2STAY.ORG © 2015

4. Positive peer community: ☐/10

It is true we grow to be like our friends. Therefore, the more time we spend with our friends, the more we will be influenced by their values and the actions that result. There are some things that parents and mentors can do to help each child and young person in the choices they make about friends.

5. Respond with compassion: ☐/10

We are acutely aware of the brokenness in the world. We all have hopes and fears about the future. Too often, we provide our children with the adult solutions to some of the world's problems rather than presenting them with the issue at hand and inviting their suggestions for what could be done.

6. Encounters with Jesus: ☐/10

Many believers can remember a time and place where they may have felt particularly close to Jesus – at an event, during a particular circumstance in their life, etc. How important it is for us to create the spaces where we can encounter the living Jesus – not just in words from the front but in the still small voice of the Spirit of God who desperately wants to communicate with each of us.

7. Big story of the Bible: ☐/10

Every part of the Bible – each event, book, character, commands, prophecy and column – must be understood in the context of one storyline. In many cases the approach to faith formation has been built around a series of disconnected Bible stories and memory verses. Kids are a part of this story – God's story. It is our privilege to help others find their place in God's big story.

8. Serve in mission: ☐ /10

Where are the opportunities for your children and young people to be able to give as they continue to grow in their journey with Jesus? When all ages can serve in the mission, there are benefits on many levels – strengthening the household of faith as well as the spiritual life of each family member.

Remember, it's not just about information. We need experiences and focus on formation that lead to the ultimate goal... transformation.

From a Church exploding with growth all around the world comes a children's ministry curriculum used in programs with 10's, 100's and 1,000's of kids.

Hillsong Kids Big is a, bible based, Jesus focussed, media rich learning experience for kids 1-12.

It's resource created by a local Church for local Churches.

Curriculum resources available from

hillsongkidsbig.com